THE SUN

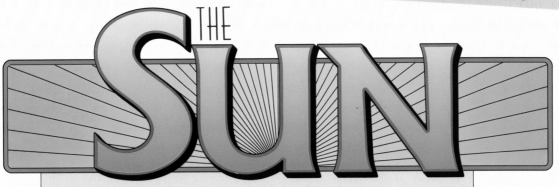

A READ-ABOUT

From earliest times, people all around the world have realized the importance of the sun and have told stories or legends about it. Many early people worshipped the sun as a god. They knew the sun was powerful.

NIGHT COMES TOO SOON!

The Maori people of New Zealand tell how the sun once used to speed across the sky. They tell how Maui snared the sun and beat it hard until the sun promised to travel more slowly.

UT THE SUN

WHERE DOES THE SUN COME FROM?

Other people believed that the sun was a golden egg laid every morning by the great goose of the sky!

WHAT IS AN ECLIPSE?

The Chinese people used to think that an eclipse was caused by a sky dragon taking bites out of the sun. When it happened, they would shout and bang drums to make the dragon spit out the sun. Sure enough, if they made enough noise, the dragon would do this, and soon the whole sun would shine once more.

On a clear dark night, you can see thousands of bright, twinkling stars. On a clear day, you can see only one star. That star is our sun. The sun is the closest star to our planet, Earth.

SUN | VENUS EARTH | MERCURY MARS | JUPITER | SATURN | URANUS | NEPTUNE PLUTO

The sun and all the other stars are huge balls of brightly burning gas spinning in the sky. Earth is a planet. It has no light of its own. Its only light comes from the sun. If we were far out in space, Earth would look like a star. This is because the sun's light would be shining on it. All the planets and our moon shine in the same way.

HOW BIG IS THE SUN?

If the sun was as big as a beach ball, our earth would be about as big as a pea! Because the sun is so far away, it seems much smaller than our earth.

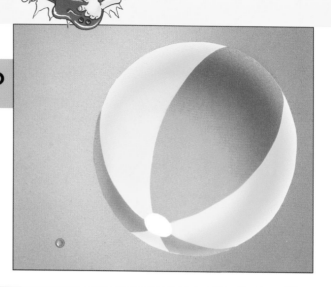

HOW FAR AWAY IS THE SUN?

The sun is about 150 million km (93 million mi) away from Earth. A spaceship speeding at 1,000 km (620 mi) an hour would take 17 years to reach the sun!

5

DAY AND NIGHT

Where does the sun go at night? The sun does not move. It is the planet Earth that moves. Our earth spins in space like a great round top, tipped a little to one side.

For about twelve hours of each day, one side of the world is facing the sun. We call these twelve hours *day*.

SUN

EARTH

SUNRISE

For the other twelve hours, that side of the world has spun away from the sun We call these twelve hours *night*.

SUNSET

THE SEASONS

The planets travel around the sun. Earth takes 365¼ days to do this. We call this travel time *one year*. Because Earth is tipped a little to one side, its travel around the sun gives Earth its seasons.

NORTHERN HEMISPHERE: JUNE
SOUTHERN HEMISPHERE: DECEMBER

DECEMBER

JUNE

NORTHERN HEMISPHERE: DECEMBER
SOUTHERN HEMISPHERE: JUNE

When one part of the earth is having winter, that part of the earth is tipped away from the sun, so the days are cooler. At the same time, the other part of the earth is tipped toward the sun and is having summer.

THE SUN - (

If the sun wasn't there, warm and bright in the sky, plants could not live on Earth.
If there were no plants, there would be no food for animals or people. Our world would be a cold, dark, lifeless place.

The green substance in leaves is called *chlorophyll*. This pigment captures the sunlight and the plant uses this energy to convert water and carbon dioxide in the air into sugar and oxygen. The process is called *photosynthesis*. All green plants refresh our air with oxygen.

The sun ripens fruit,

dries grass for hay,

makes flowers bloom,

and helps grass grow.

The sun causes the wind to blow. It heats up some parts of the earth more than others. It heats up land more than water. The air above the land is warm and rises. As it rises, cool air from over the water moves in to take its place. This causes a breeze or wind to blow.

AIR RISES OVER HOT LAND

COOL SEA BREEZE

COLD WATER

The sun's heat can be trapped in solar panels and used for power. Better use of the sun's power would save Earth's other energy resources such as oil. It is also a clean, safe source of energy and does not cause pollution.

The sun is Earth's best friend. But every day, smoke and gases rising from our cities cause pollution high above Earth.

This pollution sits like a blanket, trapping the sun's heat and making the earth warmer.

Scientists call this the *greenhouse effect*, and are concerned about the damage it will cause to our earth.

High above Earth there is the *ozone layer*, which protects us from the sun's dangerous sunburn rays.

Some gases we use are destroying the ozone layer, letting dangerous sunburn rays that cause skin cancer come down to Earth.

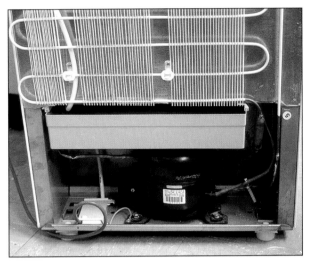

The gas that is used in fridges, freezers, and air-conditioners is very bad if it escapes into the atmosphere.

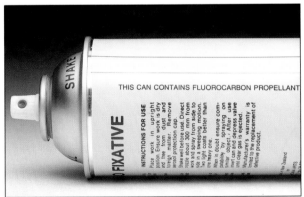

The gas that makes some spray cans squirt is very bad for the ozone layer.

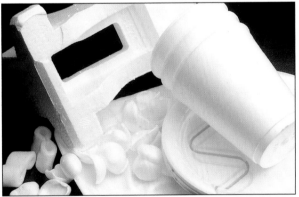

When foam packaging is burnt, dangerous gases escape into the atmosphere.

13

For many thousands of years, the sun has been Earth's friend. Now many things being done on Earth could change this. You can help stop these changes from happening if you:

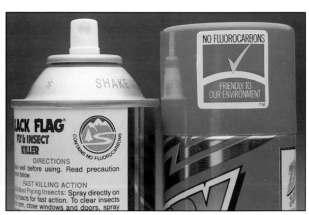

Use only spray cans that are propelled by hydrocarbons.

Plant a tree. Trees are good pollution fighters.

Talk at school about ways of stopping pollution.

Ask your parents to use lead-free fuel in the car.

Remember that the sun's rays are powerful. They can burn our skin. Always protect your skin by wearing a sunhat and sun screen.

Be the sun's friend, and it will always be yours!

INDEX